W9-CFI-060

PUMPING MAD

Edited by
Albert B. Feldstein

WARNER BOOKS

A Warner Communications Company

WARNER BOOKS EDITION

Copyright © 1973, 1974 and 1981
by E.C. Publications, Inc.

All rights reserved.
No part of this book may be reproduced without permission.
For information address E.C. Publications, Inc.,
485 Madison Avenue, New York, N.Y. 10022

Title "MAD" used with permission of its owner,
E.C. Publications, Inc.

This Warner Books Edition is published by
arrangement with E.C. Publications, Inc.

Designed by Tom Nozkowski

Warner Books, Inc.,
75 Rockefeller Plaza,
New York, N.Y. 10019

Ⓦ A Warner Communications Company

Printed in the United States of America

First Printing: February, 1981

10 9 8 7 6 5 4 3 2

Monster movies have always been good box office when they reflected the emotional climate of their time.

YECCH

or
"What a
WASTE!"

WRITER: LOU SILVERSTONE   ARTIST: DON MARTIN

Now, with the world so concerned about ecology and the environment, the new wave horror films will go something like this . . .

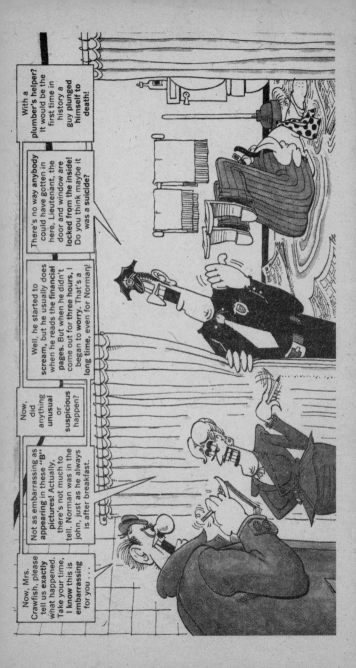

A
Witch's
Tale

THE LIGHTER SIDE OF...

MINOR

AILMENTS

ARTIST & WRITER:
DAVE BERG

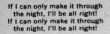

Now that the war in Vietnam is finally over . . . here is a Primer on Bowling. And if you think this is the most ridiculous introduction to a MAD article you've ever read, wait'll you read the article! Anyway, here's . . .

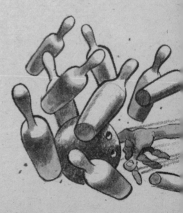

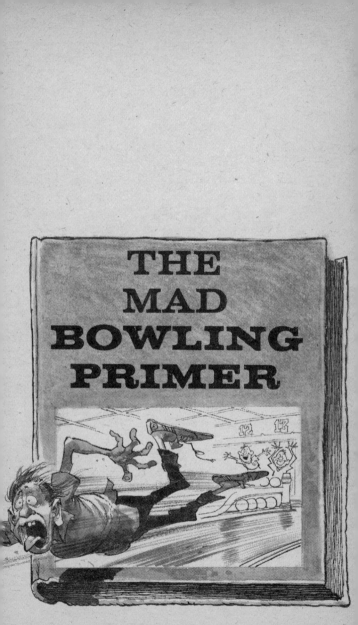

THE
MAD
BOWLING
PRIMER

ARTIST: JACK DAVIS   WRITER: LARRY SIEGEL

CHAPTER 1.

See the man.
See him drink some beer.
See him write down a score.
See him drink some more beer.
See him write another score.
See him drink some more beer.
See him walk to the foul line.
See him roll a ball.
See him walk back and drink some more beer.
In twenty minutes, he will roll another ball.
Why does the man bowl?
For the exercise!
You use a lot of muscles
Lifting beer glasses all night!

CHAPTER 2.

See the man getting ready to bowl.
He is renting Bowling Shoes.
He bowls three or four times a week.
Now look at the owner behind the counter.
Isn't he a financial wizard?
He is even smarter than Howard Hughes.
Why is he so brilliant?
We'll tell you.
Can you think of anyone else
Who can get you to spend over $50 a year
For a pair of dirty sneakers you don't even own?!

CHAPTER 3.

Most bowling alleys are automated.
In case you get into trouble,
All you have to do is push a button.
Shall we explain the buttons to you?
The button on the left is the "Reset Button."
It solves the problem of fallen pins in the alley.
The button in the center is the "Mechanic Button."
It solves the problems not covered by the "Reset Button."
The button on the right is the "Service Button."
It brings the waitress with the booze.
It won't necessarily help you with your bowling.
But it will help you forget the biggest problem of all,
Namely, that the other two buttons never work!

CHAPTER 4.

Let us teach you some "Bowling Language."
If you knock over ten pins with one ball,
That is a STRIKE.
If you knock over ten pins with two balls,
That is a SPARE.
If you knock over, say, five pins with the first ball,
And three pins with the second ball,
That is an EIGHT.
If you send the ball off the alley
So it knocks over no pins at all,
That is a %*&¢$#@#$%!!
Now you know where the expression
"Gutter Language" comes from!

CHAPTER 5.

See the girls.
They are having trouble.
They don't know how to keep score.
Ha, ha, ha, silly girls.
It is very easy to keep score in bowling.
Would you like to learn?

Okay, in the first frame, enter the amount of pins
You knock over with both balls in the first inning,
Unless you get a "Spare."
A "Spare" is 10, plus what you get on your next ball,
Which you enter in the first frame,
And add to it the total you knock over
With both balls in the second inning,
Which you enter in the second frame,
Unless you bowl another "Spare"
In which case, you repeat the procedure,
Except if you bowl a "Strike" in the first inning,
In which case, you have 10,
Plus what you get with your next two balls,
Unless the first ball of the second inning is also a "Strike",
In which case, you have 20,
But you have to wait for the third inning
To find out what you knock over with your third ball,
In order to add it to the 20, and enter it in the first frame,
And then add the second inning's 10 to that,
Plus what you get with your third and fourth balls,
And enter that in the second frame,
Unless your fourth ball is a "Strike"
In which case you repeat the procedure,
Except if you bowl a "Spare" or a "Strike" in the 10th frame,
In which case, you kill yourself!
Now, would you like to learn about the blue lines in Hockey?

CHAPTER 6.

See the bowling trophy.
This is what makes bowling worthwhile.
The trophy is being presented to Dora Grepps
For being the "Best Left-Handed Female Bowler
In The B'nai B'rith of Upper Sandusky, Ohio."
She is also the ONLY Left Handed Female Bowler
In The B'nai B'rith of Upper Sandusky, Ohio.
But that is unimportant.
The important thing is, there is no way
A bowler can do anything in a Bowling Center
Without getting a trophy.
See how excited Mrs. Grepps is with her new trophy.
She's so excited, she has to go to the Ladies Room.
When she is finished,
The matron will give her a towel,
And a bar of soap,
And another trophy.

CHAPTER 7.

See the League Bowling competition.
Isn't it exciting?
All the greats and near-greats of Industry are here.
Look, there's the team from "Al's Service Station",
And the gang from "Barney's Moving and Storage",
And the boys from "Cy's Poultry Market".
See the team in the fourth alley.
They have just finished a game.
Their combined score is 421.
But when they submit their score sheet
It will read "792"...
Do you find that hard to understand?
That's the team from "Chuck's TV Repair Shop"!
Now do you understand?

CHAPTER 8.

What's going on here?
It is a "Celebrity Bowling Show."
Famous stars bowl against each other,
And make awful jokes,
And engage in witless horseplay.
Is there anything more asinine and idiotic
Than making us watch people like Dean Martin,
And Efram Zimbalist, Jr., and Johnny Carson,
And Joey Bishop, and Sonny and Cher
On a TV Bowling Show?
Only one thing we can think of!
Making us watch them on their *own* TV shows!

CHAPTER 9.

See the Bowling Center on Sunday.
See all the Fathers and Sons,
And Fathers and Daughters.
Is there a "Father and Son League"
Or a "Father and Daughter League"?
Not exactly.
Sundays are Visiting Days for Divorced Men.
Split, split, split!
Since most Fathers do not know
What to do on Visting Days,
They take their kids bowling.
Which is more than they did
When they lived at home!

A MAD
CITY STREET SCENE
WE'D LIKE TO SEE

ARTIST: GEORGE WOODBRIDGE

WRITER: LOU SILVERSTONE

A MAD SUBURBAN STREET SCENE WE'D LIKE TO SEE

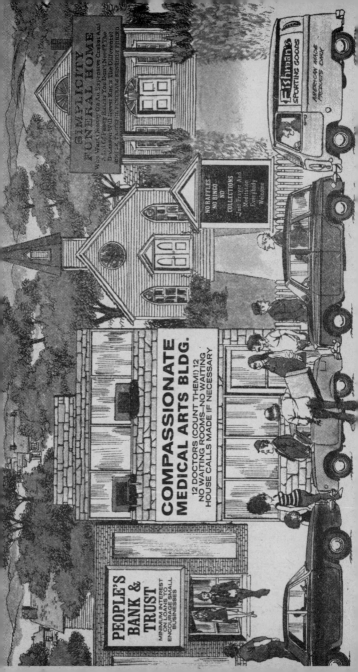

Whenever we buy a bottle of cough medicine or a can of soup, there's a label on it that lists all the ingredients. That's so we'll know what's inside, and we won't be fooled by the outside appearance. Unfortunately, our lives are affected by people more than bottles and cans, and you can never tell exactly what's inside them. So wouldn't it be a good idea

If People Were Labeled Like Products

ARTIST: BOB CLARKE   WRITER: FRANK JACOBS

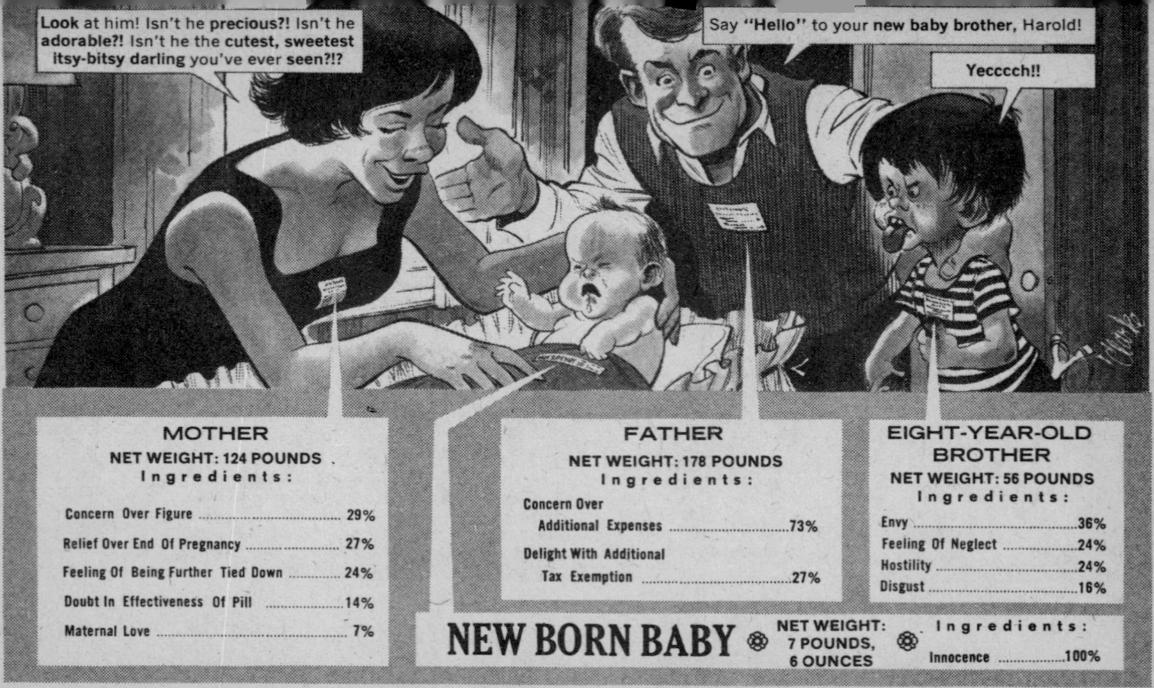
Look at him! Isn't he precious?! Isn't he adorable?! Isn't he the cutest, sweetest itsy-bitsy darling you've ever seen?!?
Say "Hello" to your new baby brother, Harold!
Yeccccch!!
MOTHER
NET WEIGHT: 124 POUNDS
Ingredients:
Concern Over Figure 29%
Relief Over End Of Pregnancy 27%
Feeling Of Being Further Tied Down 24%
Doubt In Effectiveness Of Pill 14%
Maternal Love 7%
FATHER
NET WEIGHT: 178 POUNDS
Ingredients:
Concern Over Additional Expenses 73%
Delight With Additional Tax Exemption 27%
EIGHT-YEAR-OLD BROTHER
NET WEIGHT: 56 POUNDS
Ingredients:
Envy 36%
Feeling Of Neglect 24%
Hostility 24%
Disgust 16%
NEW BORN BABY
NET WEIGHT: 7 POUNDS, 6 OUNCES
Ingredients:
Innocence 100%

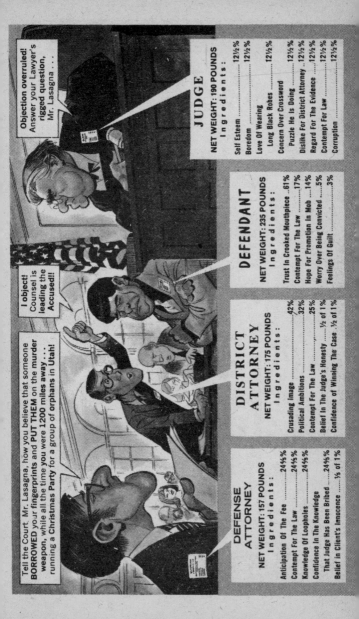

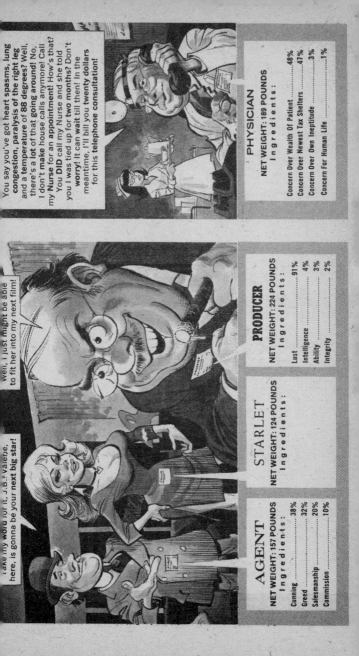

Did I ever tell you the one about the Polack with a speech impediment—or was it an Italian with a harelip? In any case, Riley goes into Schultz's Tavern and meets Cohen... or is it the other way around? Whatever! The bartender— I think his name was Jack—looks at the Black guy, and says...uh...Aw, heck, I forget the punchline! But I got another one! It seems there were these two Hungarians who married a pair of Siamese twins! Well, one night...

Ahh! How exquisite you look! What a joy eet eez for Pierre to bring out zee true beauty of zee real you! Fortunately, you are zo gorgeous to begin weeth!

BORE
NET WEIGHT: 193 POUNDS
Ingredients:

Long Windedness	38%
Self Centeredness	34%
Additives	25%
Sensitivity	2%
Taste	1%

VICTIM
NET WEIGHT: 148 POUNDS
Ingredients:

Politeness	7%
Distress	9%
Resentment	11%
Boredom	13%
Masochism	60%

Beautician
NET WEIGHT: 147 POUNDS
Ingredients:

Flattery	15%
Pretentiousness	17%
Combined Drivel, Bunk, Tripe, Rot and Prattle	18%
Inne Hatred Of Women	50%

BEAUTY SHOP PATRON
NET WEIGHT: 132 POUNDS
Ingredients:

Vanity	20%
Self-Delusion	20%
Naive Hope	20%
Wash, Rinse, Bleach and	

A MODERN
FAIRY TALE

ARTIST & WRITER: SERGIO ARAGONES

Here we go with another vital MAD Public Service Feature
... this one designed to instruct you in the tricky art of

INTERPRETING THE NEWS

WRITER: GARY ALEXANDER

WHAT THEY SAY...

... today, a White House spokesman revealed ...

... first reports had indicated ...

... and after a long investigation ...

... vows to remain on the job ...

... a relentless effort will be made to find the killer ...

... has offered no comment ...

... surveillance has been increased ...

... but terms of the contract have not been disclosed ...

... are calling the blaze suspicious ...

... has introduced a bill into Congress which would effect far-reaching reforms ...

... faces a maximum penalty of 20 years in prison ...

WHAT IT MEANS...

... today, a White House spokesman finally revealed what everybody else already knew ...

... first reports were all wrong ...

... a Stoolie finally came through ...

... everybody wants him off the job ...

... there's no chance of ever finding the killer ...

... is too embarrassed to comment ...

... they still haven't found anything ...

... the Rank and File will get the short end again ...

... looks like the Arsonist got away ...

... the Congress will defeat a bill which would have effected far-reaching reforms ...

... will get 6 months, with a suspended sentence ...

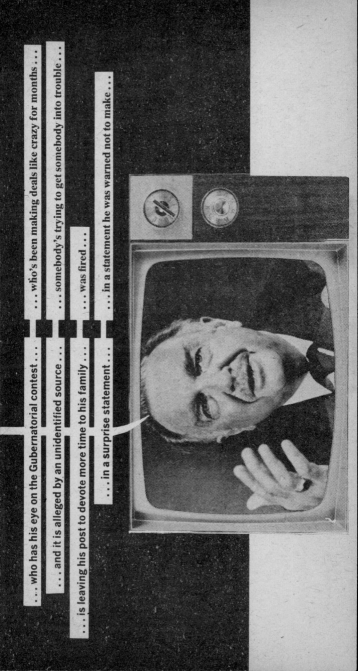

What's been just about the biggest thing going in the movies for the past couple of years? Nostalgia, right? The film-makers took us back to the 1920's in "The Boy Friend", to the '30's in "Paper Moon", to the '40's in "Summer of '42", and to the '50's in "The Last Picture Show". So that just about uses up all the important nostalgia decades, and now on to other things, right? Wrong!

Hi! Welcome to a typical small town in California! The year is 1962, and we're four average teenagers! I'd like to let you know exactly what's going to happen in this movie! First of all, we're gonna do a lot of cruisin' in our bitchin' wheels! That means riding around in our great cars! We're gonna have run-ins with Holsteins! That means the Police! We're gonna fool around with boss babes! That means gorgeous girls! And we're gonna bore you clean out of your minds with the most meaningless, idiotic night you've ever seen in you life! And that means exactly what it sounds like it means!

My name is Squirt! I'm a sensitive intellectual! I drive an average of 200 miles a night up and down Main Street! My ambition is to make out with a chick in a white T-Bird who I never met! And the man I admire most in the world is the town disc jockey, Werewolf Wally! Well, here in California, that's a sensitive intellectual!!!

My name is Steed! I'm in love with Squirt's sister, Borey! Tomorrow, Squirt and I are supposed to leave for college in the East! Borey wants me to stay here, marry her, and go to UCLA! But my High School grades aren't good enough to get me into a California college! I . . . I flunked Surfing!

I'm Yawn! I'm also in love! But not with some dopey High School kid! My love is deeper and more meaningful! I'm in love with a 1958 Mercedes! I know it sounds ridiculous, but if we can work out our religious differences, who knows . . . ?

My name is Terrier! I'm the square in the crowd! And, boy . . . have I got problems! First of all, I look like **David Eisenhower!** Come to think of it, with a problem like that, the others are unimportant!

My name is Jimmy! I'm not really in this picture! But, just for a change, I thought somebody out there might like to see a nice, old familiar face on the screen!

Some producer has just discovered another decade! What else? The 1960's! Okay, all you nostalgic 12-year-olds out there, it's time now to go back to the "Soaring Sixties" and reminisce over your glorious past—just a few minutes ago. So bring out the banners, fall into line, and get ready to march in one more parade down "Memory Lane, U.S.A." ...while we here at MAD start tossing

ARTIST:
MORT DRUCKER

WRITER:
LARRY SIEGEL

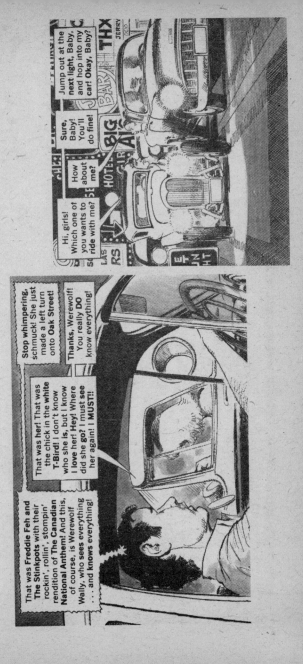

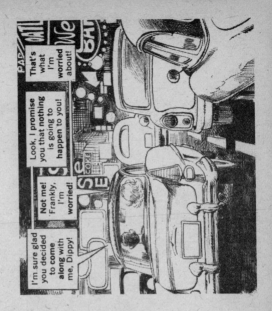

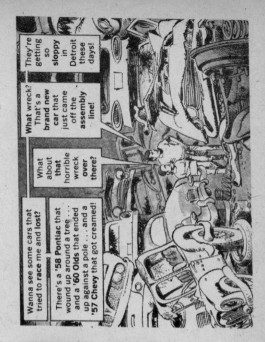

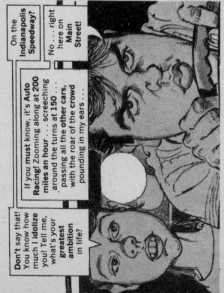

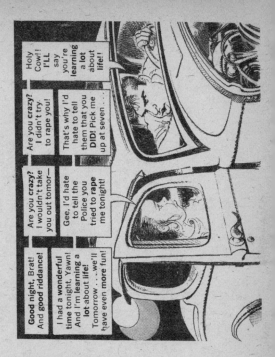

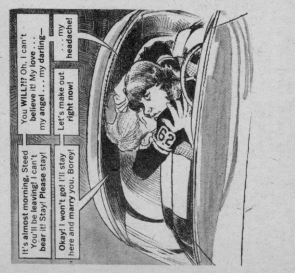

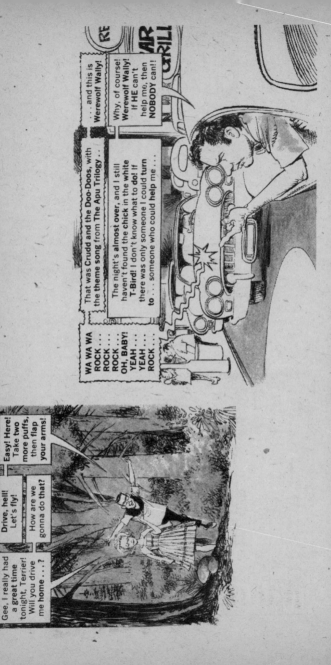

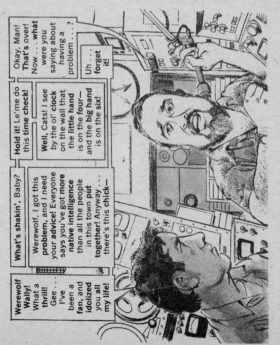

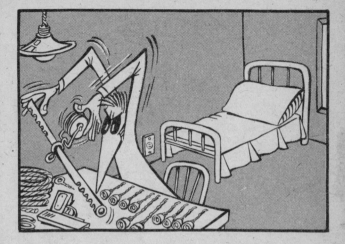

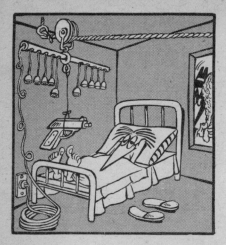

MAD VISITS THE "REALISTIC SCHOOL OF MEDICINE"

ARTIST: PAUL COKER, JR.   WRITER: LARRY SIEGEL

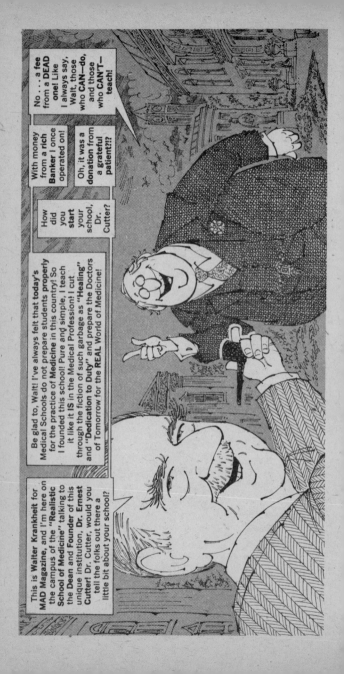

Now, here's an interesting course at the **Realistic School of Medicine**, which is important to all future Doctors! Here, they learn to write their **Bills!**

... now then, we take the Patient's income, which let's say is **$15,000,** and we take him for 10% of that, or **$1,500!** Then we add **$25** each time we step into his room, even though he's in the Hospital anyway! For argument's sake, that's **$250** more! Then we determine how much Blue Shield will pay him for **Surgery!** Let's say, it's **$1000!** So we add, let's say, another **$1000** to our bill on general principles. Then we . . .

And what do you call this course?

It's listed in our program as **"Medical Math,"** but we refer to it as **"Fantasy and Science Fiction"!**

I notice that you have a **blind student** at the school!

Yes . . . that's **Cranby!** He's also **deaf** and **mute!**

Deaf, dumb and blind! What's he **DOING** here?

Studying to be an Insurance Exam Doctor! He'll make out fine!

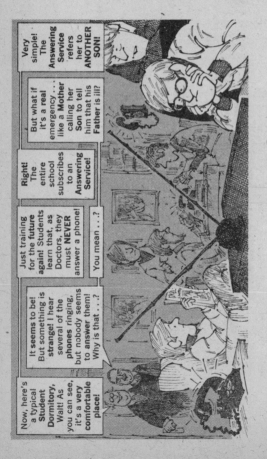

A MAD LOOK AT

MARRIAGE

• • •

BEFORE

AND

AFTER

ARTIST: JACK RICKARD   WRITER: GEORGE HART

THE LIGHTER SIDE OF...

CRIME IN THE STREETS

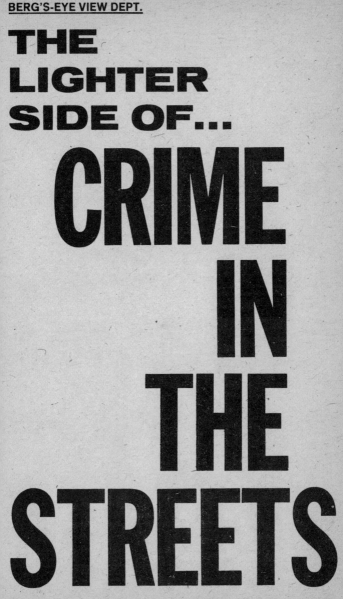

ARTIST & WRITER: DAVE BERG

A MAD LOOK AT KARATE

ARTIST & WRITER: SERGIO ARAGONÉS

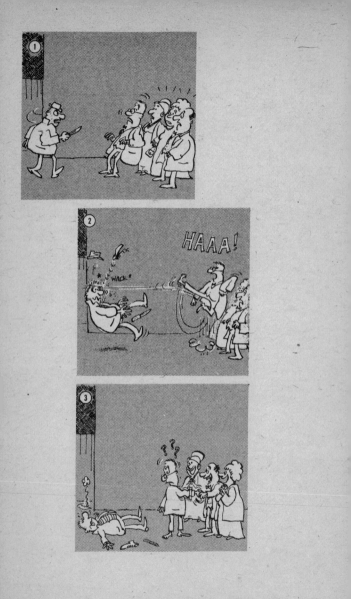

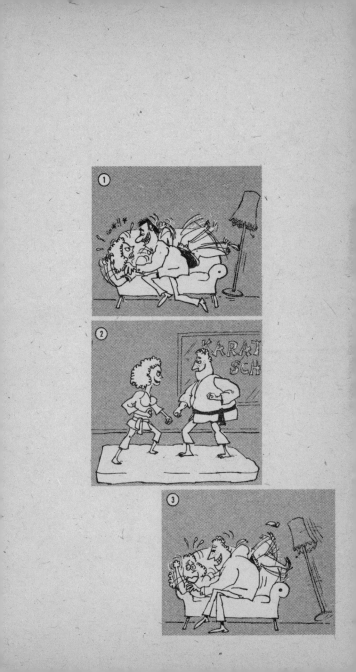

THERE SEEMS to be a basic instinct that drives us to flaunt Status Symbols so the world will know what clever and superior members of the herd we really are. And, although there has never been anything commendable about Status Symbols, at least we all knew what they were as we clawed our way up the ladder from Status Symbol Roller Skates with lots of extra ball bearings to Status Symbol limousines with lots of extra cylinders.

But recently, the marks of Status have changed in every age group. Suddenly, the whole neat orderly garish system has been upset. Today, the Status Symbols of adults are regarded as tasteless by the younger generation, whose funky treasures are in turn condemned by the small fry as being just plain icky. And so, because MAD thinks it would be a shame if its industrious readers continued lying, cheating and stealing to reach the top, only to flaunt the wrong Status Symbol after they got there, and to help all of you to become the envy of the low class peasants you are forced to associate with, we have called upon a costly imported writer and a uniquely hand-carved expensive artist to prepare this

A
MAD
GUIDE
TO
STATUS
SYMBOLS

ARTIST: PAUL COKER, JR.   WRITER: TOM KOCH

WHEN YOU'RE A LITTLE KID...

A $200 dog that can win blue ribbons is not a Status Symbol.

A 50c lizard that can make girls scream is.

Breaking your arm climbing trees is not a Status Symbol.

Breaking your leg playing football is.

A Twinkie in your lunch box is not a Status Symbol.

An Energy Wafer like the Astronauts eat is.

Having an ancestor who was a British nobleman is not a Status Symbol.

Having one who was a Blackfoot Indian Chief is.

Owning a de luxe, jumbo box of 36 crayons is not a Status Symbol.

Eating all of them on a dare at recess is.

WHEN YOU'RE A BIGGER KID...

Being able to buy lunch for friends is not a Status Symbol.

Being able to scrounge lunch from strangers is.

Breaking your leg playing football is no longer a Status Symbol.

Breaking both your legs skiing is.

Imported shoes are not a Status Symbol.

Bare feet, either imported or domestic, are.

WHEN YOU'RE A YOUNG ADULT...

Breaking one or two bones in some juvenile pastime is not a Status Symbol.

Breaking all of your bones sky-diving is.

A 1974 VW with automatic shift is not a Status Symbol.

A 1954 VW with psychedelic paint is.

Flunking your Algebra Test is not a Status Symbol.

Flunking your Wasserman Test isn't one either.

Dressing poor when you're rich is a Status Symbol.

Dressing poor because you really are poor isn't.

*Holding your
Sweet Sixteen
Party in a hotel
ballroom is not
a Status Symbol.*

*Holding it in
a condemned
warehouse
or a junked
bus is.*

Going to a psychiatrist is not a Status Symbol.

Going to a guru who worships wax fruit is.

WHEN YOU'RE A VERY OLD (OVER 30) ADULT...

Being jailed for slapping your wife is not a Status Symbol.

Being jailed for clubbing a lettuce grower is.

Breaking any or all of your bones is not a Status Symbol.

Acquiring a tennis elbow is.

A diploma from Vassar is not a Status Symbol.

A diploma from the Tel Aviv Academy of Tractoring is.

Having your books audited by the I.R.S. is not a Status Symbol.

Having your mail screened by the F.B.I. is.

Owning A-rated stocks is not a Status Symbol.

Producing X-rated movies is.

Working in a ghetto one day a week is a Status Symbol.

Living there seven days a week is not.

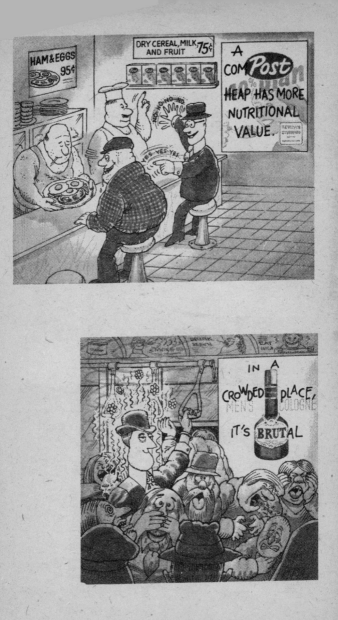

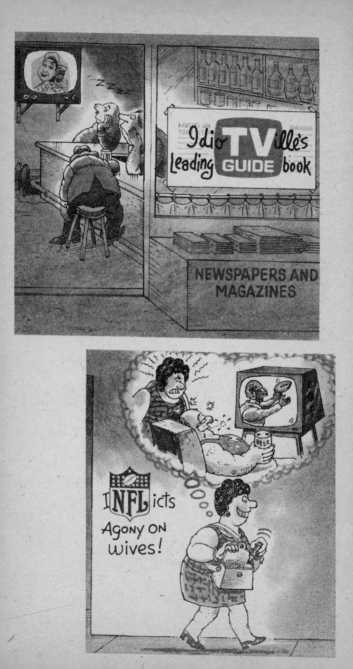

might happen if those Graffiti Rascals ever started attacking that holy of holies, the Corporate Signature. Here are some of the horrors (heh-heh!) that could occur with

MARK FITI

ARTIST & WRITER:
AL JAFFEE

AN IRRESISTIBLE TEMPTATION TO STATUS-SEEKING SOCIAL CLIMBERS

Spray cans and magic markers are changing the face of America. Every day, new bits of irreverence are added to trains, buses, buildings, billboards and any other available public surface. We at MAD shudder to think what

Daddy, why do we have bad things, like a **Depression**?

A Depression isn't **all** bad, Merry-Girl! Like, it helps bring folks **closer together**!

It sure does!

Daddy, the **bathroom pipe** broke, and the floor's knee-deep in—

Stranger, you happen t' know anythin' about plumbing?

HEY! Where in heck you **goin'**?

T' the Salvation Army! THEY give you somethin' t' eat an' a place t' sleep . . . an' all you gotto do THERE is listen t' a couple of lousy HYMNS!!

with the revolutionary new approach to TV Program-
no private-eyes, no crime, no bloodshed . . . just a sweet,
ing to death during the Great Depression, and life was

Dulltons

If the Good Lord intended for us t' **have** a phone He would've put one in our **bodies** instead of an **appendix!**

Even if we **can't** phone a Doctor, it's comforting to know that we live in a time when a Doctor will **come** to our house if somebody is sick!

I was **thinkin'** . . . what's the good of **havin'** a Doctor who'll make **House Calls,** when he'll only go to folks who can **pay**—and everybody around here is **BROKE?!?**

ARTIST: ANGELO TORRES   WRITER: LOU SILVERSTONE

Here we go with MAD's version of the new TV series ming . . . no violence, no action, no controversy, no cops, simple, nostalgic look at the days when people were starv-dull . . . dull . . . dull! Like it is watching

The

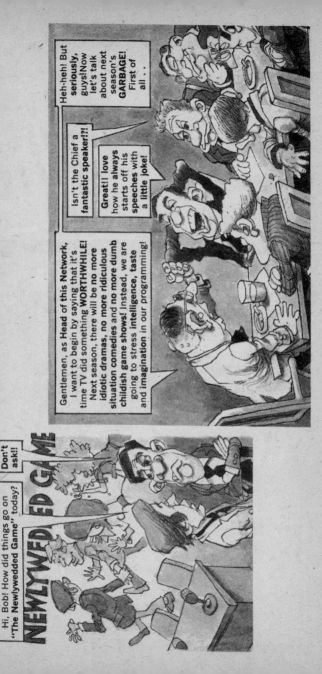

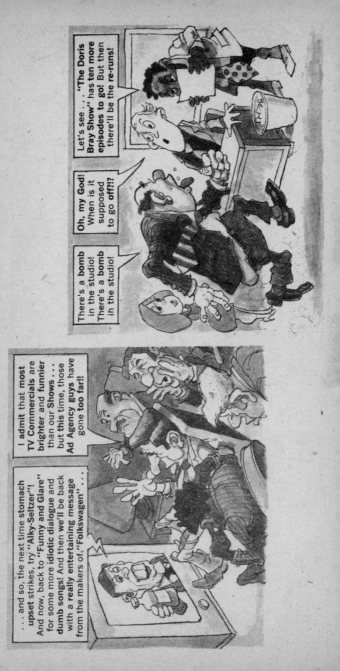

Do you have any tickets for any TV Shows?
Yes, Sir! I have one for "Bernie Loves Midgets"! That'll be ten dollars!!
I thought TV Show tickets were FREE! I'm not paying ten dollars to see that awful piece of junk!
But you don't pay US! We pay YOU!!
Forget it!
Er . . . Fifteen dollars!
Okay, twenty dollars! And after the show, you get a free visit to the best stomach specialist in town!
But don't you see? No human system could possibly survive that show!
How do you know?
Because I'm the best stomach specialist in town!
KNBZ
TELEVISION

Owning a profitable factory is not a Status Symbol.

Owning an unprofitable football team is.

Living in a 200-year old farmhouse is a Status Symbol.

Living in a 50-year old Apartment house is not.

A MAD PEEK BEHIND THE SCENES AT A TV NETWORK

ARTIST: BRUCE DAY
WRITER: LARRY SIEGEL